PENGUIN BOOKS

SELECTED POEMS: CAROL ANN DUFFY

Born in Glasgow in 1955, Carol Ann Duffy grew up in
Staffordshire and attended university in Liverpool. Her poetry has
been highly praised and she has received many awards. In 1984
she won an Eric Gregory Award, and she has been a recipient of a
Scottish Arts Council Book Award for her collections *Standing
Female Nude* and *The Other Country*. Carol Ann Duffy was
awarded a Somerset Maugham Award in 1988 for her collection
Selling Manhattan, the Dylan Thomas Award in 1989 and a
Cholmondeley Award in 1992. Her collection of poems *Mean
Time* was also awarded a Scottish Arts Council Book Award, and
won the 1993 Whitbread Award for Poetry and the Forward
Prize. *Rapture* won the 2006 T. S. Eliot Prize. She has edited two
anthologies for teenagers, *I Wouldn't Thank You for a Valentine*
and *Stopping for Death*. Carol Ann Duffy was awarded an OBE
in the 1995 Birthday Honours List. She has one daughter, and
lives in Manchester.

Carol Ann Duffy

Selected Poems

PENGUIN BOOKS
in association with
ANVIL PRESS POETRY LTD

PENGUIN BOOKS

Published by the Penguin Group
Penguin Books Ltd, 80 Strand, London WC2R 0RL, England
Penguin Group (USA) Inc., 375 Hudson Street, New York, New York 10014, USA
Penguin Group (Canada), 90 Eglinton Avenue East, Suite 700, Toronto, Ontario, Canada M4P 2Y3
(a division of Pearson Penguin Canada Inc.)
Penguin Ireland, 25 St Stephen's Green, Dublin 2, Ireland (a division of Penguin Books Ltd)
Penguin Group (Australia), 250 Camberwell Road, Camberwell,
Victoria 3124, Australia (a division of Pearson Australia Group Pty Ltd)
Penguin Books India Pvt Ltd, 11 Community Centre,
Panchsheel Park, New Delhi – 110 017, India
Penguin Group (NZ), cnr Airborne and Rosedale Roads, Albany,
Auckland 1310, New Zealand (a division of Pearson New Zealand Ltd)
Penguin Books (South Africa) (Pty) Ltd, 24 Sturdee Avenue,
Rosebank, Johannesburg 2196, South Africa

Penguin Books Ltd, Registered Offices: 80 Strand, London WC2R 0RL, England

www.penguin.com

Standing Female.Nude first published by Anvil Press Poetry 1985
Selling Manhattan first published by Anvil Press Poetry 1987
The Other Country first published by Anvil Press Poetry 1990
Mean Time first published by Anvil Press Poetry 1993
The World's Wife first published by Picador 1999
This selection first published in Penguin Books 1994
Reissued 2006
10

ISBN-13: 978-0-141-02512-4

www.greenpenguin.co.uk

Contents

From **The Other Country** (*1990*)

From **Mean Time** (*1993*)

From **The World's Wife** (*1999*)

From **Standing Female Nude** (*1985*)

Girl Talking

On our Eid day my cousin was sent to
the village. Something happened. We think it was pain.
She gave wheat to the miller and the miller
gave her flour. Afterwards it did not hurt,
so for a while she made chapatis. *Tasleen*,
said her friends, *Tasleen, do come out with us.*

They were in a coy near the swing. It's like
a field. Sometimes we planted melons, spinach,
marrow, and there was a well. She sat on the swing.
They pushed her till she shouted *Stop the swing*,
then she was sick. Tasleen told them to find
help. She made blood beneath the mango tree.

Her mother held her down. She thought something
was burning her stomach. We paint our hands.
We visit. We take each other money.
Outside, the children played Jack-with-Five-Stones.
Each day she'd carried water from the well
into the Mosque. Men washed and prayed to God.

After an hour she died. Her mother cried.
They called a Holy Man. He walked from Dina
to Jhang Chak. He saw her dead, then said

She went out at noon and the ghost took her heart.
From that day we were warned not to do this.
Baarh is a small red fruit. We guard our hearts.

Comprehensive

Tutumantu is like hopscotch, Kwani-kwani is like hide-
 and-seek.
When my sister came back to Africa she could only
 speak
English. Sometimes we fought in bed because she didn't
 know
what I was saying. I like Africa better than England.
My mother says You will like it when we get our own
 house.
We talk a lot about the things we used to do
in Africa and then we are happy.

Wayne. Fourteen. Games are for kids. I support
the National Front. Paki-bashing and pulling girls'
knickers down. Dad's got his own mini-cab. We watch
the video. I Spit on Your Grave. Brilliant.
I don't suppose I'll get a job. It's all them
coming over here to work. Arsenal.

Masjid at 6 o'clock. School at 8. There was
a friendly shop selling rice. They ground it at home
to make the evening nan. Families face Mecca.
There was much more room to play than here in
 London.
We played in an old village. It is empty now.

We got a plane to Heathrow. People wrote to us
that everything was easy here.

It's boring. Get engaged. Probably work in Safeways
worst luck. I haven't lost it yet because I want
respect. Marlon Frederic's nice but he's a bit dark.
I like Madness. The lead singer's dead good.
My mum is bad with her nerves. She won't
let me do nothing. Michelle. It's just boring.

Ejaz. They put some sausages on my plate.
As I was going to put one in my mouth
a Moslem boy jumped on me and pulled.
The plate dropped on the floor and broke. He asked me
    in Urdu
if I was a Moslem. I said Yes. You shouldn't be eating
    this.
It's a pig's meat. So we became friends.

My sister went out with one. There was murder.
I'd like to be mates, but they're different from us.
Some of them wear turbans in class. You can't help
taking the piss. I'm going in the Army.
No choice really. When I get married
I might emigrate. A girl who can cook
with long legs. Australia sounds all right.

Some of my family are named after the Moghul
    emperors.
Aurangzeb, Jehangir, Batur, Humayun. I was born
thirteen years ago in Jhelum. This is a hard school.
A man came in with a milk crate. The teacher told us

to drink our milk. I didn't understand what she was
   saying,
so I didn't go to get any milk. I have hope and am
   ambitious.
At first I felt as if I was dreaming, but I wasn't.
Everything I saw was true.

Head of English

Today we have a poet in the class.
A real live poet with a published book.
Notice the inkstained fingers girls. Perhaps
we're going to witness verse hot from the press.
Who knows. Please show your appreciation
by clapping. Not too loud. Now

sit up straight and listen. Remember
the lesson on assonance, for not all poems,
sadly, rhyme these days. Still. Never mind.
Whispering's, as always, out of bounds –
but do feel free to raise some questions.
After all, we're paying forty pounds.

Those of you with English Second Language
see me after break. We're fortunate
to have this person in our midst.
Season of mists and so on and so forth.
I've written quite a bit of poetry myself,
am doing Kipling with the Lower Fourth.

Right. That's enough from me. On with the Muse.
Open a window at the back. We don't
want winds of change about the place.
Take notes, but don't write reams. Just an essay

on the poet's themes. Fine. Off we go.
Convince us that there's something we don't know.

Well. Really. Run along now girls. I'm sure
that gave an insight to an outside view.
Applause will do. Thank you
very much for coming here today. Lunch
in the hall? Do hang about. Unfortunately
I have to dash. Tracey will show you out.

Lizzie, Six

What are you doing?
I'm watching the moon.
I'll give you the moon
when I get up there.

Where are you going?
To play in the fields.
I'll give you fields,
bend over that chair.

What are you thinking?
I'm thinking of love.
I'll give you love
when I've climbed this stair.

Where are you hiding?
Deep in the wood.
I'll give you wood
when your bottom's bare.

Why are you crying?
I'm afraid of the dark.
I'll give you the dark
and I do not care.

Education for Leisure

Today I am going to kill something. Anything.
I have had enough of being ignored and today
I am going to play God. It is an ordinary day,
a sort of grey with boredom stirring in the streets.

I squash a fly against the window with my thumb.
We did that at school. Shakespeare. It was in
another language and now the fly is in another
     language.
I breathe out talent on the glass to write my name.

I am a genius. I could be anything at all, with half
the chance. But today I am going to change the world.
Something's world. The cat avoids me. The cat
knows I am a genius, and has hidden itself.

I pour the goldfish down the bog. I pull the chain.
I see that it is good. The budgie is panicking.
Once a fortnight, I walk the two miles into town
for signing on. They don't appreciate my autograph.

There is nothing left to kill. I dial the radio
and tell the man he's talking to a superstar.
He cuts me off. I get our bread-knife and go out.
The pavements glitter suddenly. I touch your arm.

I Remember Me

There are not enough faces. Your own gapes back
at you on someone else, but paler, then the moment
when you see the next one and forget yourself.

It must be dreams that make us different, must be
private cells inside a common skull.
One has the other's look and has another memory.

Despair stares out from tube-trains at itself
running on the platform for the closing door. Everyone
you meet is telling wordless barefaced truths.

Sometimes the crowd yields one you put a name to,
snapping fiction into fact. Mostly your lover passes
in the rain and does not know you when you speak.

Whoever She Was

They see me always as a flickering figure
on a shilling screen. Not real. My hands,
still wet, sprout wooden pegs. I smell the apples
burning as I hang the washing out.
Mummy, say the little voices of the ghosts
of children on the telephone. Mummy.

A row of paper dollies, cleaning wounds
or boiling eggs for soldiers. The chant
of magic words repeatedly. I do not know.
Perhaps tomorrow. If we're very good.
The film is on a loop. Six silly ladies
torn in half by baby fists. When they
think of me, I'm bending over them at night
to kiss. Perfume. Rustle of silk. Sleep tight.

Where does it hurt? A scrap of echo clings
to the bramble bush. My maiden name
sounds wrong. This was the playroom.
I turn it over on a clumsy tongue. Again.
These are the photographs. Making masks
from turnips in the candlelight. In case they come.

Whoever she was, forever their wide eyes watch her
as she shapes a church and steeple in the air.

She cannot be myself and yet I have a box
of dusty presents to confirm that she was here.
You remember the little things. Telling stories
or pretending to be strong. Mummy's never wrong.
You open your dead eyes to look in the mirror
which they are holding to your mouth.

Dear Norman

I have turned the newspaper boy into a diver
for pearls. I can do this. In my night
there is no moon, and if it happens that I speak
of stars it's by mistake. Or if it happens
that I mention these things, it's by design.

His body is brown, breaking through waves. Such white
 teeth.
Beneath the water he searches for the perfect shell.
He does not know that, as he posts the *Mirror*
through the door, he is equal with dolphins.
I shall name him Pablo, because I can.

Pablo laughs and shakes the seaweed from his hair.
Translucent on his palm a pearl appears. He is
 reminded.
Cuerpo de mujer, blancas colinas, muslos blancos.
I find this difficult, and then again easy,
as I watch him push his bike off in the rain.

As I watch him push his bike off in the rain
I trace his name upon the window-pane.
There is little to communicate, but I have rearranged

the order of the words. Pablo says You want for me
to dive again? I want for you to dive.

Tomorrow I shall deal with the dustman.

Talent

This is the word *tightrope*. Now imagine
a man, inching across it in the space
between our thoughts. He holds our breath.

There is no word *net*.

You want him to fall, don't you?
I guessed as much; he teeters but succeeds.
The word *applause* is written all over him.

$

A one a two a one two three four –
boogie woogie chou chou cha cha chatta
noogie. Woogie wop a loo bop a wop
bim bam. Da doo ron a doo ron oo wop a
sha na? Na na hey hey doo wah did.
Um, didy ay didy shala lala lala lala,
boogie woogie choo choo cha cha bop.
(A woogie wop a loo bam) yeah yeah yeah.

Liverpool Echo

Pat Hodges kissed you once, although quite shy,
in sixty-two. Small crowds in Mathew Street
endure rain for the echo of a beat,
as if nostalgia means you did not die.

Inside phone-booths loveless ladies cry
on Merseyside. Their faces show defeat.
An ancient jukebox blares out *Ain't She Sweet*
in Liverpool, which cannot say goodbye.

Here everybody has an anecdote
of how they met you, were the best of mates.
The seagulls circle round a ferry-boat

out on the river, where it's getting late.
Like litter on the water, people float
outside the Cavern in the rain. And wait.

Standing Female Nude

Six hours like this for a few francs.
Belly nipple arse in the window light,
he drains the colour from me. Further to the right,
Madame. And do try to be still.
I shall be represented analytically and hung
in great museums. The bourgeoisie will coo
at such an image of a river-whore. They call it Art.

Maybe. He is concerned with volume, space.
I with the next meal. You're getting thin,
Madame, this is not good. My breasts hang
slightly low, the studio is cold. In the tea-leaves
I can see the Queen of England gazing
on my shape. Magnificent, she murmurs,
moving on. It makes me laugh. His name

is Georges. They tell me he's a genius.
There are times he does not concentrate
and stiffens for my warmth.
He possesses me on canvas as he dips the brush
repeatedly into the paint. Little man,
you've not the money for the arts I sell.
Both poor, we make our living how we can.

I ask him Why do you do this? Because
I have to. There's no choice. Don't talk.
My smile confuses him. These artists
take themselves too seriously. At night I fill myself
with wine and dance around the bars. When it's
     finished
he shows me proudly, lights a cigarette. I say
Twelve francs and get my shawl. It does not look like
     me.

Oppenheim's Cup and Saucer

She asked me to luncheon in fur. Far from
the loud laughter of men, our secret life stirred.

I remember her eyes, the slim rope of her spine.
This is your cup, she whispered, and this mine.

We drank the sweet hot liquid and talked dirty.
As she undressed me, her breasts were a mirror

and there were mirrors in the bed. She said Place
your legs around my neck, that's right. Yes.

Shooting Stars

After I no longer speak they break our fingers
to salvage my wedding ring. Rebecca Rachel Ruth
Aaron Emmanuel David, stars on all our brows
beneath the gaze of men with guns. Mourn for the
     daughters,

upright as statues, brave. You would not look at me.
You waited for the bullet. Fell. I say Remember.
Remember these appalling days which make the world
for ever bad. One saw I was alive. Loosened

his belt. My bowels opened in a ragged gape of fear.
Between the gap of corpses I could see a child.
The soldiers laughed. Only a matter of days separate
this from acts of torture now. They shot her in the eye.

How would you prepare to die, on a perfect April
     evening
with young men gossiping and smoking by the graves?
My bare feet felt the earth and urine trickled
down my legs until I heard the click. Not yet. A trick.

After immense suffering someone takes tea on the lawn.
After the terrible moans a boy washes his uniform.
After the history lesson children run to their toys the
    world
turns in its sleep the spades shovel soil Sara Ezra . . .

Sister, if seas part us, do you not consider me?
Tell them I sang the ancient psalms at dusk
inside the wire and strong men wept. Turn thee
unto me with mercy, for I am desolate and lost.

The Dolphins

World is what you swim in, or dance, it is simple.
We are in our element but we are not free.
Outside this world you cannot breathe for long.
The other has my shape. The other's movement
forms my thoughts. And also mine. There is a man
and there are hoops. There is a constant flowing
   guilt.

We have found no truth in these waters,
no explanations tremble on our flesh.
We were blessed and now we are not blessed.
After travelling such space for days we began
to translate. It was the same space. It is
the same space always and above it is the man.

And now we are no longer blessed, for the world
will not deepen to dream in. The other knows
and out of love reflects me for myself.
We see our silver skin flash by like memory
of somewhere else. There is a coloured ball
we have to balance till the man has disappeared.

The moon has disappeared. We circle well-known
   grooves
of water on a single note. Music of loss forever

from the other's heart which turns my own to stone.
There is a plastic toy. There is no hope. We sink
to the limits of this pool until the whistle blows.
There is a man and our mind knows we will die here.

A Healthy Meal

The gourmet tastes the secret dreams of cows
tossed lightly in garlic. Behind the green door, swish
of oxtails languish on an earthen dish. Here are
wishbones and pinkies; fingerbowls will absolve guilt.

Capped teeth chatter to a kidney or at the breast
of something which once flew. These hearts knew
no love and on their beds of saffron rice they lie
beyond reproach. What is the claret like? Blood.

On table six, the language of tongues is braised
in armagnac. The woman chewing suckling pig
must sleep with her husband later. Leg,
saddle and breast bleat against pure white cloth.

Alter *calf* to *veal* in four attempts. This is
the power of words; knife, tripe, lights, charcuterie.
A fat man orders his *rare* and a fine sweat
bastes his face. There are napkins to wipe the evidence

and sauces to gag the groans of abattoirs. The menu
lists the recent dead in French, from which they order
offal, poultry, fish. Meat flops in the jowls. Belch.
Death moves in the bowels. You are what you eat.

And Then What

Then with their hands they would break bread
wave choke phone thump thread

Then with their tired hands slump
at a table holding their head

Then with glad hands hold other hands
or stroke brief flesh in a kind bed

Then with their hands on the shovel
they would bury their dead.

From **Selling Manhattan** *(1987)*

Dies Natalis

When I was cat, my mistress tossed me sweetmeats
from her couch. Even the soldiers were deferential –
she thought me sacred – I saw my sleek ghost
arch in their breastplates and I purred

my one eternal note beneath the shadow of pyramids.
The world then was measured by fine wires
which had their roots in my cat brain, trembled
for knowledge. She stroked my black pelt, singing

her different, frantic notes into my ear.
These were meanings I could not decipher. Later,
my vain, furred tongue erased a bowl of milk,
then I slept and fed on river rats . . .

She would throw pebbles at the soil, searching
with long, gold nails for logic in chaos;
or bathe at night in the moon's pool,
dissolving its light into wobbling pearls.

I was there, my collar of jewels and eyes shining,
my small heart impartial. Even now, at my spine's base,
the memory of a tail stirs idly, defining that night.
Cool breeze. Eucalyptus. Map of stars above

which told us nothing, randomly scattered like pebbles.
The man who feared me came at dawn, fought her
until she moaned into stillness, her ringed hand
with its pattern of death, palm up near my face.

*

Then a breath of sea air after blank decades,
my wings applauding this new shape. Far below,
the waves envied the sky, straining for blueness,
muttering in syllables of fish. I trod air, laughing,

what space was salt was safe. A speck became a ship,
filling its white sails like gulping lungs. Food swam.
I swooped, pincered the world in my beak, then soared
across the sun. The great whales lamented the past

wet years away, sending their bleak songs back
and forth between themselves. I hovered, listening,
as water slowly quenched fire. My cross on the surface
followed, marking where I was in the middle of
     nowhere . . .

Six days later found me circling the ship. Men's voices
came over the side in scraps. I warned patiently
in my private language, weighed down with loneliness.
Even the wind had dropped. The sea stood still,

flicked out its sharks, and the timber wheezed.
I could only be bird, as the wheel of the day turned
     slowly
between sun and moon. When night fell, it was stale,
unbearably quiet, holding the breath of the dead.

The egg was in my gut, nursing its own deaths
in a delicate shell. I remember its round weight
persistently pressing; opening my bowel onto the deck
near a young sailor, the harsh sound my cry made
    then.

                *

But when I loved, I thought that was all I had done.
It was very ordinary, an ordinary place, the river
filthy, and with no sunset to speak of. She spoke
in a local accent, laughing at mine, kissed

with her tongue. This changed me. *Christ, sweetheart,*
marry me. I'll go mad. A dog barked. She ran off,
teasing, and back down the path came *Happen you*
    will . . .
Afterwards, because she asked, I told her my prospects,

branded her white neck. She promised herself
in exchange for a diamond ring. The sluggish water
shrugged past as we did it again. We whispered
false vows which would ruin our lives . . .

I cannot recall more pain. There were things one could
    buy
to please her, but she kept herself apart, spitefully
guarding the password. My body repelled her. Sweat.
Sinew. All that had to be hunched away in nylon sheets.

We loathed in the same dull air till silver presents came,
our two hands clasping one knife to cut a stale cake.
    One day,
the letter. Surgery. When the treatment did not work,
she died. I cried over the wishbone body, wondering

what was familiar, watching myself from a long way
    off.
I carried the remains in an urn to the allotment,
trying to remember the feel of her, but it was years,
years, and what blew back in my face was grey ash,
    dust.

                              *

Now hushed voices say I have my mother's look.
Once again, there is light. The same light. I talk
to myself in shapes, though something is constantly
    changing
the world, rearranging the face which stares at mine.

Most of the time I am hungry, sucking on dry air
till it gives in, turning milky and warm. Sleep
is dreamless, but when I awake I have more
to contemplate. They are trying to label me,

translate me into the right word. My small sounds
bring a bitter finger to my mouth, a taste
which cannot help or comfort me. I recall
and release in a sigh the journey here . . .

The man and woman are different colours and I
am both of them. These strangers own me,
pass me between them chanting my new name. They
    wrap
and unwrap me, a surprise they want to have again,

mouthing their tickly love to my smooth, dark flesh.
The days are mosaic, telling a story for the years
to come. I suck my thumb. New skin thickens
on my skull, to keep the moments I have lived before

locked in. I will lose my memory, learn words
which barely stretch to cover what remains unsaid.
    Mantras
of consolation come from those who keep my portrait
in their eyes. And when they disappear, I cry.

The Dummy

Balancing me with your hand up my back, listening
to the voice you gave me croaking for truth, you keep
me at it. Your lips don't move, but your eyes look
desperate as hell. Ask me something difficult.

Maybe we could sing together? Just teach me
the right words, I learn fast. Don't stare like that.
I'll start where you leave off. I can't tell you
anything if you don't throw me a cue line. We're dying

a death right here. Can you dance? No. I don't suppose
you'd be doing this if you could dance. Right? Why do
  you
keep me in that black box? I can ask questions too,
you know. I can see that worries you. Tough.

So funny things happen to everyone on the way to most
  places.
Come on. You can do getter than that, can't you?

Model Village

See the cows placed just so on the green hill.
Cows say *Moo*. The sheep look like little clouds,
don't they? Sheep say *Baa*. Grass is green
and the pillar-box is red. Wouldn't it be strange
if grass were red? This is the graveyard
where the villagers bury their dead. Miss Maiden
lives opposite in her cottage. She has a cat.
The cat says *Miaow*. What does Miss Maiden say?

I poisoned her, but no one knows. Mother, I said,
drink your tea. Arsenic. Four sugars. He waited
years for me, but she had more patience. One day,
he didn't come back. I looked in the mirror,
saw her grey hair, her lips of reproach. I found
the idea in a paperback. I loved him, you see,
who never so much as laid a finger. Perhaps now
you've learnt your lesson, she said, pouring
another cup. Yes, Mother, yes. Drink it all up.

The white fence around the farmyard
looks as though it's smiling. The hens are tidying
the yard. Hens say *Cluck* and give us eggs. Pigs
are pink and give us sausages. *Grunt*, they say.
Wouldn't it be strange if hens laid sausages?
Hee-haw, says the donkey. The farmhouse

is yellow and shines brightly in the sun. Notice
the horse. Horses say *Neigh*. What does the Farmer say?

To tell the truth, it haunts me. I'm a simple man,
not given to fancy. The flock was ahead of me,
the dog doing his job like a good'un. Then
I saw it. Even the animals stiffened in fright. Look,
I understand the earth, treat death and birth
the same. A fistful of soil tells me plainly
what I need to know. You plant, you grow, you reap.
But since then, sleep has been difficult. When I shovel
deep down, I'm searching for something. Digging, desperately.

There's the church and there's the steeple.
Open the door and there are the people. Pigeons
roost in the church roof. Pigeons say *Coo*.
The church bells say *Ding-dong*, calling
the faithful to worship. What God says
can be read in the Bible. See the postman's dog
waiting patiently outside church. *Woof*, he says.
Amen, say the congregation. What does Vicar say?

Now they have all gone, I shall dress up
as a choirboy. I have shaved my legs. How smooth
they look. Smooth, pink knees. If I am not good,
I shall deserve punishment. Perhaps the choirmistress
will catch me smoking behind the organ. A good boy
would own up. I am naughty. I can feel
the naughtiness under my smock. Smooth, pink naughtiness.
The choirmistress shall wear boots and put me
over her lap. I tremble and dissolve into childhood.

Quack, say the ducks on the village pond. Did you
see the frog? Frogs say *Croak*. The village-folk shop
at the butcher's, the baker's, the candlestick maker's.
The Grocer has a parrot. Parrots say *Pretty Polly*
and *Who's a pretty boy then?* The Vicar is nervous
of parrots, isn't he? Miss Maiden is nervous
of Vicar and the Farmer is nervous of everything.
The library clock says *Tick-tock*. What does the
    Librarian say?

Ssssh. I've seen them come and go over the years,
my ears tuned for every whisper. This place
is a refuge, the volumes breathing calmly
on their still shelves. I glide between them
like a doctor on his rounds, know their cases. Tomes
do no harm, here I'm safe. Outside is chaos,
lives with no sense of plot. Behind each front door
lurks truth, danger. I peddle fiction. Believe
you me, the books in everyone's head are stranger . . .

Recognition

Things get away from one.
I've let myself go, I know.
Children? I've had three
and don't even know them.

I strain to remember a time
when my body felt lighter.
Years. My face is swollen
with regrets. I put powder on,

but it flakes off. I love him,
through habit, but the proof
has evaporated. He gets upset.
I tried to do all the essentials

on one trip. Foolish, yes,
but I was weepy all morning.
Quiche. A blond boy swung me up
in his arms and promised the earth.

You see, this came back to me
as I stood on the scales.
I wept. Shallots. In the window,
creamy ladies held a pose

which left me clogged and old.
The waste. I'd forgotten my purse,
fumbled; the shopgirl gaped at me,
compassionless. Claret. I blushed.

Cheese. Kleenex. *It did happen.*
I lay in my slip on wet grass,
laughing. Years. I had to rush out,
blind in a hot flush, and bumped

into an anxious, dowdy matron
who touched the cold mirror
and stared at me. Stared
and said I'm sorry sorry sorry.

And How Are We Today?

The little people in the radio are picking on me
again. It is sunny, but they are going to make it
rain. I do not like their voices, they have voices
like cold tea with skin on. I go O O O.

The flowers are plastic. There is all dust
on the petals. I go Ugh. Real flowers die,
but at least they are a comfort to us all.
I know them by name, listen. Rose. Tulip. Lily.

I live inside someone else's head. He hears me
with his stethoscope, so it is no use
sneaking home at five o'clock to his nice house
because I am in his ear going Breathe Breathe.

I might take my eye out and swallow it
to bring some attention to myself. Winston did.
His name was in the paper. For the time being
I make noises to annoy them and then I go
    BASTARDS.

Psychopath

I run my metal comb through the D.A. and pose
my reflection between dummies in the window at
   Burton's.
Lamp light. Jimmy Dean. All over town, ducking and
   diving,
my shoes scud sparks against the night. She is in the
   canal.
Let me make myself crystal. With a good-looking girl
   crackling
in four petticoats, you feel like a king. She rode past
   me
on a wooden horse, laughing, and the air sang *Johnny,
Remember Me*. I turned the world faster, flash.

I don't talk much. I swing up beside them and do it
with my eyes. Brando. She was clean. I could smell her.
I thought, Here we go, old son. The fairground spun
   round us
and she blushed like candyfloss. You can woo them
with goldfish and coconuts, whispers in the Tunnel of
   Love.
When I zip up the leather, I'm in a new skin, I touch it
and love myself, sighing Some little lady's going to get
   lucky
tonight. My breath wipes me from the looking-glass.

We move from place to place. We leave on the last
    morning
with the scent of local girls on our fingers. They wear
our lovebites on their necks. I know what women want,
a handrail to Venus. She said *Please* and *Thank you*
to the toffee-apple, teddy-bear. I thought I was on, no
    error.
She squealed on the dodgems, clinging to my leather
    sleeve.
I took a swig of whisky from the flask and frenched it
down her throat. *No*, she said, *Don't*, like they always
    do.

Dirty Alice flicked my dick out when I was twelve.
She jeered. I nicked a quid and took her to the spinney.
I remember the wasps, the sun blazing as I pulled
her knickers down. I touched her and I went hard,
but she grabbed my hand and used that, moaning . . .
She told me her name on the towpath, holding the fish
in a small sack of water. We walked away from the
    lights.
She'd come too far with me now. She looked back,
    once.

A town like this would kill me. A gypsy read my palm.
She saw fame. I could be anything with my looks,
my luck, my brains. I bought a guitar and blew a smoke
    ring
at the moon. Elvis nothing. *I'm not that type*, she said.

Too late. I eased her down by the dull canal
and talked sexy. Useless. She stared at the goldfish,
    silent.
I grabbed the plastic bag. She cried as it gasped and
    wriggled
on the grass and here we are. A dog craps by a
    lamp-post.

Mama, straight up, I hope you rot in hell. The old man
sloped off, sharpish. I saw her through the kitchen
    window.
The sky slammed down on my school cap, chicken
    licken.
Lady, Sweetheart, Princess, I say now, but I never stay.
My sandwiches were near her thigh, then the Rent Man
lit her cigarette and I ran, ran . . . She is in the canal.
These streets are quiet, as if the town has held its breath
to watch the Wheel go round above the dreary homes.

No, don't. Imagine. One thump did it, then I was on
    her,
giving her everything I had. Jack the Lad, Ladies' Man.
Easier to say Yes. Easier to stay a child, wide-eyed
at the top of the helter-skelter. You get one chance in
    this life
and if you screw it you're done for, uncle, no mistake.
She lost a tooth. I picked her up, dead slim, and slid her
    in.
A girl like that should have a paid-up solitaire and high
    hopes,
but she asked for it. A right well-knackered outragement.

My reflection sucks a sour Woodbine and buys me a
    drink. Here's

looking at you. Deep down I'm talented. She found
    out. Don't mess

with me, angel, I'm no nutter. Over in the corner, a
    dead ringer

for Ruth Ellis smears a farewell kiss on the lip of a gin-
    and-lime.

The barman calls Time. Bang in the centre of my skull,

there's a strange coolness. I could almost fly.

    Tomorrow

will find me elsewhere, with a loss of memory. Drink
    up son,

the world's your fucking oyster. A wopbopaloobop
    alopbimbam.

Selling Manhattan

All yours, Injun, twenty-four bucks' worth of glass beads,
gaudy cloth. I got myself a bargain. I brandish
fire-arms and fire-water. Praise the Lord.
Now get your red ass out of here.

I wonder if the ground has anything to say.
You have made me drunk, drowned out
the world's slow truth with rapid lies.
But today I hear again and plainly see. Wherever
you have touched the earth, the earth is sore.

I wonder if the spirit of the water has anything
to say. That you will poison it. That you
can no more own the rivers and the grass than own
the air. I sing with true love for the land;
dawn chant, the song of sunset, starlight psalm.

Trust your dreams. No good will come of this.
My heart is on the ground, as when my loved one
fell back in my arms and died. I have learned
the solemn laws of joy and sorrow, in the distance
between morning's frost and firefly's flash at night.

Man who fears death, how many acres do you need
to lengthen your shadow under the endless sky?
Last time, this moment, now, a boy feels his freedom

vanish, like the salmon going mysteriously
out to sea. Loss holds the silence of great stones.

I will live in the ghost of grasshopper and buffalo.

The evening trembles and is sad.
A little shadow runs across the grass
and disappears into the darkening pines.

Stealing

The most unusual thing I ever stole? A snowman.
Midnight. He looked magnificent; a tall, white mute
beneath the winter moon. I wanted him, a mate
with a mind as cold as the slice of ice
within my own brain. I started with the head.

Better off dead than giving in, not taking
what you want. He weighed a ton; his torso,
frozen stiff, hugged to my chest, a fierce chill
piercing my gut. Part of the thrill was knowing
that children would cry in the morning. Life's tough.

Sometimes I steal things I don't need. I joy-ride cars
to nowhere, break into houses just to have a look.
I'm a mucky ghost, leave a mess, maybe pinch a
    camera.
I watch my gloved hand twisting the doorknob.
A stranger's bedroom. Mirrors. I sigh like this – *A ah*.

It took some time. Reassembled in the yard,
he didn't look the same. I took a run
and booted him. Again. Again. My breath ripped out
in rags. It seems daft now. Then I was standing
alone amongst lumps of snow, sick of the world.

Boredom. Mostly I'm so bored I could eat myself.
One time, I stole a guitar and thought I might
learn to play. I nicked a bust of Shakespeare once,
flogged it, but the snowman was strangest.
You don't understand a word I'm saying, do you?

The Virgin Punishing the Infant

after the painting by Max Ernst

He spoke early. Not the *goo goo goo* of infancy,
but *I am God*. Joseph kept away, carving himself
a silent Pinocchio out in the workshed. He said
he was a simple man and hadn't dreamed of this.

She grew anxious in that second year, would stare
at stars saying *Gabriel? Gabriel?* Your guess.
The village gossiped in the sun. The child was solitary,
his wide and solemn eyes could fill your head.

After he walked, our normal children crawled. Our
    wives
were first resentful, then superior. Mary's child
would bring her sorrow . . . better far to have a son
who gurgled nonsense at your breast. *Googoo. Googoo.*

But *I am God*. We heard him through the window,
heard the smacks which made us peep. What we saw
was commonplace enough. But afterwards, we
    wondered
why the infant did not cry. And why the Mother did.

Big Sue and *Now, Voyager*

Her face is a perfect miniature on wide, smooth flesh,
    flesh,
a tiny fossil in a slab of stone. Most evenings
Big Sue is Bette Davis. Alone. The curtains drawn.
The TV set an empty head which has the same
recurring dream. Mushrooms taste of kisses. Sherry
    trifle
is a honeymoon. *Be honest. Who'd love me?*

Paul Henreid. He lights two cigarettes and, gently,
puts one in her mouth. The little flat in Tooting
is a floating ship. Violins. Big Sue drawing deeply
on a chocolate stick. *Now, Voyager, depart. Much,*
much for thee is yet in store. Her eyes are wider,
bright. The precious video unspools the sea.

This is where she lives, the wrong side of the glass
in black-and-white. To press the rewind,
replay, is to know perfection. Certainty. The soundtrack
drowns out daytime echoes. *Size of her. Great cow.*
Love is never distanced into memory, persists
unchanged. Oscar-winners looking at the sky.

Why wish for the moon? Outside the window night falls,
slender women rush to meet their dates. Men whistle

on the dark blue streets at shapes they want
or, in the pubs, light cigarettes for two. Big Sue
unwraps a Mars Bar, crying at her favourite scene.
The bit where Bette Davis says *We have the stars.*

Foreign

Imagine living in a strange, dark city for twenty years.
There are some dismal dwellings on the east side
and one of them is yours. On the landing, you hear
your foreign accent echo down the stairs. You think
in a language of your own and talk in theirs.

Then you are writing home. The voice in your head
recites the letter in a local dialect; behind that
is the sound of your mother singing to you,
all that time ago, and now you do not know
why your eyes are watering and what's the word for
    this.

You use the public transport. Work. Sleep. Imagine one
    night
you saw a name for yourself sprayed in red
against a brick wall. A hate name. Red like blood.
It is snowing on the streets, under the neon lights,
as if this place were coming to bits before your eyes.

And in the delicatessen, from time to time, the coins
in your palm will not translate. Inarticulate,
because this is not home, you point at fruit. Imagine
that one of you says *Me not know what these people mean.*
It like they only go to bed and dream. Imagine that.

Correspondents

When you come on Thursday, bring me a letter. We
    have
the language of stuffed birds, teacups. We don't have
the language of bodies. My husband will be here.
I shall inquire after your wife, stirring his cup
with a thin spoon, and my hand shall not tremble.
Give me the letter as I take your hat. Mention
the cold weather. My skin burns at the sight of you.

We skim the surface, gossip. I baked this cake and you
eat it. Words come from nowhere, drift off
like the smoke from his pipe. Beneath my dress, my
    breasts
swell for your lips, belly churns to be stilled
by your brown hands. This secret life is Gulliver,
held down by strings of pleasantries. I ache. Later
your letter flares up in the heat and is gone.

Dearest Beloved, pretend I am with you . . . I read
your dark words and do to myself things
you can only imagine. I hardly know myself.
Your soft, white body in my arms . . . When we part,
you kiss my hand, bow from the waist, all passion

patiently restrained. *Your servant, Ma'am*. Now you
   write
wild phrases of love. The words blur as I cry out once.

Next time we meet, in drawing-room or garden,
passing our letters cautiously between us, our eyes
fixed carefully on legal love, think of me here
on my marriage-bed an hour after you've left.
I have called your name over and over in my head
at the point your fiction brings me to. I have kissed
your sweet name on the paper as I knelt by the fire.

Telegrams

URGENT WHEN WE MEET COMPLETE STRANGERS
DEAR STOP
THOUGH I COUNT THE HOURS TILL YOU ARE NEAR
STOP
WILL EXPLAIN LATER DATE TILL THEN CANT
WAIT STOP C

COMPLETELY FOGGED WHAT DO YOU MEAN BABY?
STOP
CANT WE SLOPE OFF TO MY PLACE MAYBE? STOP
NOT POSS ACT NOT MET WITH RAISON DETRE
STOP B

FOR GODS SAKE JUST TRUST ME SWEETHEART
STOP
NATCH IT HURTS ME TOO WHEN WERE APART
STOP
SHIT WILL HIT FAN UNLESS STICK TO PLAN STOP
C

SHIT? FAN? TRUST? WHATS GOING ON HONEY?
STOP
IF THIS IS A JOKE IT ISNT FUNNY STOP
INSIST ON TRUTH LOVE YOU BUT STRUTH! STOP B

YES I KNOW DARLING I LOVE YOU TOO STOP
TRY TO SEE PREDIC FROM MY POINT OF VIEW
    STOP
IF YOU DONT PLAY BALL I WONT COME AT ALL
    STOP C

PLEASE REPLY LAST TELEGRAM STOP
HAVE YOU FORGOTTEN THAT NIGHT IN
    MATLOCK? C

NO WAS TRYING TO TEACH YOU LESSON PET STOP
ALSO BECAUSE OF THESE AM IN DEBT STOP
TRUST WHEN NEXT MEET WILL PASSIONATELY
    GREET STOP B

NO NO NO NO GET IT THROUGH YOUR THICK
    HEAD STOP
IF SEEN WITH YOU AM AS GOOD AS DEAD STOP
THE WIFE WILL GUESS WEVE BEEN HAVING SEX
    STOP C

SO YOURE MARRIED? HA! I MIGHT HAVE GUESSED
    STOP
THOUGHT IT ODD YOU WORE STRING VEST STOP
AS SOON AS I MET YOU I WENT OVER THE TOP
NOW DO ME A FAVOUR PLEASE PLEASE STOP STOP
    B

Lovesick

I found an apple.
A red and shining apple.
I took its photograph.

I hid the apple in the attic.
I opened the skylight
and the sun said *Ah!*

At night, I checked that it was safe,
under the giggling stars,
the sly moon. My cool apple.

Whatever you are calling about,
I am not interested.
Go away. You with the big teeth.

Warming Her Pearls

for Judith Radstone

Next to my own skin, her pearls. My mistress
bids me wear them, warm then, until evening
when I'll brush her hair. At six, I place them
round her cool, white throat. All day I think of
   her,

resting in the Yellow Room, contemplating silk
or taffeta, which gown tonight? She fans herself
whilst I work willingly, my slow heat entering
each pearl. Slack on my neck, her rope.

She's beautiful. I dream about her
in my attic bed; picture her dancing
with tall men, puzzled by my faint, persistent scent
beneath her French perfume, her milky stones.

I dust her shoulders with a rabbit's foot,
watch the soft blush seep through her skin
like an indolent sigh. In her looking-glass
my red lips part as though I want to speak.

Full moon. Her carriage brings her home. I see
her every movement in my head . . . Undressing,
taking off her jewels, her slim hand reaching
for the case, slipping naked into bed, the way

she always does . . . And I lie here awake,
knowing the pearls are cooling even now
in the room where my mistress sleeps. All night
I feel their absence and I burn.

Miles Away

I want you and you are not here. I pause
in this garden, breathing the colour thought is
before language into still air. Even your name
is a pale ghost and, though I exhale it again
and again, it will not stay with me. Tonight
I make you up, imagine you, your movements clearer
than the words I have you say you said before.

Wherever you are now, inside my head you fix me
with a look, standing here whilst cool late light
dissolves into the earth. I have got your mouth wrong,
but still it smiles. I hold you closer, miles away,
inventing love, until the calls of nightjars
interrupt and turn what was to come, was certain,
into memory. The stars are filming us for no one.

From **The Other Country** (*1990*)

Originally

We came from our own country in a red room
which fell through the fields, our mother singing
our father's name to the turn of the wheels.
My brothers cried, one of them bawling *Home,
Home,* as the miles rushed back to the city,
the street, the house, the vacant rooms
where we didn't live any more. I stared
at the eyes of a blind toy, holding its paw.

All childhood is an emigration. Some are slow,
leaving you standing, resigned, up an avenue
where no one you know stays. Others are sudden.
Your accent wrong. Corners, which seem familiar,
leading to unimagined, pebble-dashed estates, big
    boys
eating worms and shouting words you don't
    understand.
My parents' anxiety stirred like a loose tooth
in my head. *I want our own country,* I said.

But then you forget, or don't recall, or change,
and, seeing your brother swallow a slug, feel only
a skelf of shame. I remember my tongue
shedding its skin like a snake, my voice

in the classroom sounding just like the rest. Do I only
   think
I lost a river, culture, speech, sense of first space
and the right place? Now, *Where do you come from?*
strangers ask. *Originally?* And I hesitate.

In Mrs Tilscher's Class

You could travel up the Blue Nile
with your finger, tracing the route
while Mrs Tilscher chanted the scenery.
Tana. Ethiopia. Khartoum. Aswân.
That for a hour, then a skittle of milk
and the chalky Pyramids rubbed into dust.
A window opened with a long pole.
The laugh of a bell swung by a running child.

This was better than home. Enthralling books.
The classroom glowed like a sweetshop.
Sugar paper. Coloured shapes. Brady and Hindley
faded, like the faint, uneasy smudge of a mistake.
Mrs Tilscher loved you. Some mornings, you found
she'd left a good gold star by your name.
The scent of a pencil slowly, carefully, shaved.
A xylophone's nonsense heard from another form.

Over the Easter term, the inky tadpoles changed
from commas into exclamation marks. Three frogs
hopped in the playground, freed by a dunce,
followed by a line of kids, jumping and croaking
away from the lunch queue. A rough boy

told you how you were born. You kicked him, but
    stared
at your parents, appalled, when you got back home.

That feverish July, the air tasted of electricity.
A tangible alarm made you always untidy, hot,
fractious under the heavy, sexy sky. You asked her
how you were born and Mrs Tilscher smiled,
then turned away. Reports were handed out.
You ran through the gates, impatient to be grown,
as the sky split open into a thunderstorm.

Weasel Words

It was explained to Sir Robert Armstrong that
'weasel words' are 'words empty of meaning, like an
egg which has had its contents sucked out by a weasel'.

Let me repeat that we Weasels mean no harm.
You may have read that we are vicious hunters,
but this is absolutely not the case. Pure bias
on the part of your Natural History Book. *Hear, hear.*

We are long, slim-bodied carnivores with exceptionally
short legs and we have never denied this.
Furthermore, anyone here today could put a Weasel
down his trouser-leg and nothing would happen. *Weasel*
    laughter.

Which is more than can be said for the Ferrets opposite.
You can trust a Weasel, let me continue, a Weasel
does not break the spinal cord of its victim with one
    bite.
Weasel cheers. Our brown fur coats turn white in winter.

And as for eggs, here is a whole egg. It looks like an
    egg.
It is an egg. *Slurp.* An egg. *Slurp.* A whole egg. *Slurp*
    ... Slurp ...

Poet for Our Times

I write the headlines for a Daily Paper.
It's just a knack one's born with all-right-Squire.
You do not have to be an educator,
just bang the words down like they're screaming *Fire!*
CECIL-KEAYS ROW SHOCK TELLS EYETIE WAITER.
ENGLAND FAN CALLS WHINGEING FROG A LIAR.

Cheers. Thing is, you've got to grab attention
with just one phrase as punters rush on by.
I've made mistakes too numerous to mention,
so now we print the buggers inches high.
TOP MP PANTIE ROMP INCREASES TENSION.
RENT BOY: ROCK STAR PAID ME WELL TO LIE.

I like to think that I'm a sort of poet
for our times. My shout. Know what I mean?
I've got a special talent and I show it
in punchy haikus featuring the Queen.
DIPLOMAT IN BED WITH SERBO-CROAT.
EASTENDERS' BONKING SHOCK IS WELL-OBSCENE.

Of course, these days, there's not the sense of panic
you got a few years back. What with the box
et cet. I wish I'd been around when the Titanic
sank. To headline that, mate, would've been the tops.

SEE PAGE 3 TODAY GENTS THEY'RE GIGANTIC.
KINNOCK-BASHER MAGGIE PULLS OUT STOPS.

And, yes, I have a dream – make that a scotch, ta –
that kids will know my headlines off by heart.
IMMIGRANTS FLOOD IN CLAIMS HEATHROW WATCHER.
GREEN PARTY WOMAN IS A NIGHTCLUB TART.
The poems of the decade . . . *Stuff 'em! Gotcha!*
The instant tits and bottom line of art.

Making Money

Turnover. Profit. Readies. Cash. Loot. Dough. Income.
  Stash.
Dosh. Bread. Finance. Brass. I give my tongue over
to money; the taste of warm rust in a chipped mug
of tap-water. Drink some yourself. Consider
an Indian man in Delhi, Salaamat the *niyariwallah*,
who squats by an open drain for hours, sifting shit
for the price of a chapati. More than that. His hands
in crumbling gloves of crap pray at the drains
for the pearls in slime his grandfather swore he found.

Megabucks. Wages. Interest. Wealth. I sniff and snuffle
for a whiff of pelf; the stench of an abattoir blown
by a stale wind over the fields. Roll up a fiver,
snort. Meet Kim. Kim will give you the works,
her own worst enema, suck you, lick you, squeal
red weals to your whip, be nun, nurse, nanny,
nymph on a credit card. Don't worry.
Kim's only in it for the money. Lucre. Tin. Dibs.

I put my ear to brass lips; a small fire's whisper
close to a forest. Listen. His cellular telephone
rings in the Bull's car. Golden hello. Big deal. Now get
  this
straight. *Making a living is making a killing these days.*

Jobbers and brokers buzz. He paints out a landscape
by number. The Bull. Seriously rich. Nasty. One of us.

Salary. Boodle. Oof. Blunt. Shekels. Lolly. Gelt. Funds.
I wallow in coin, naked; the scary caress of a fake hand
on my flesh. Get stuck in. Bergama. The boys from the
    bazaar
hide on the target-range, watching the soldiers fire.
    Between bursts,
they rush for the spent shells, cart them away for scrap.
Here is the catch. Some shells don't explode. Ahmat
runs over grass, lucky for six months, so far. So
bomb-collectors die young. But the money's good.

Palmgrease. Smackers. Greenbacks. Wads. I widen my
    eyes
at a fortune; a set of knives on black cloth, shining,
utterly beautiful. Weep. The economy booms
like cannon, far out at sea on a lone ship. We leave
our places of work, tired, in the shortening hours, in
    the time
of night our town could be anywhere, and some of us
    pause
in the square, where a clown makes money swallowing
    fire.

Descendants

Most of us worked the Lancashire vineyards all year
                     and a few freak redheads died.
We were well-nuked. Knackered. The gaffers gave us a
                     bonus
in Burgdy and Claray. Big fucking deal, we thought,
                     we'd been robbing them blind
for months. Drink enough of it, you can juggle with
                     snakes, no sweat.

Some nights, me and Sarah went down to the ocean
                     with a few flasks
and a groundsheet and we'd have it off three or four
                     times in a night
that barely got dark. For hours, you could hear the
                     dolphins rearing up
as if they were after something. Strange bastards. I like
                     dolphins.

Anyway. She's soft, Sarah. She can read. Big green
                     moon and her with a book
of *poetry* her Gran had. Nuke me. Nice words, right
                     enough, and I love the girl,
but I'd had plenty. *Winter*, I goes, *Spring, Autumn,*
                     Summer, don't give me

that crap, Sarah, and I flung the book over the white
                              sand, into the waves,
beyond the dolphins. Click-click. Sad. I hate the bastard
                                        past, see,
I'd piss on an ancestor as soon as trace one. *What
                         fucking seasons*
I says to her, *just look at us now*. So we looked. At each
                                             other.
At the trembling unsafe sky. And she started, didn't
                              she, to cry.
Tears over her lovely blotchy purple face. It got to me.

Liar

She made things up: for example, that she was really
a man. After she'd taken off her cotton floral
day-frock she was him all right, in her head,
dressed in that heavy herringbone from Oxfam.
He was called Susan actually. The eyes in the mirror
knew that, but she could stare them out.

Of course, a job; of course, a humdrum city flat;
of course, the usual friends. Lover? Sometimes.
She lived like you do, a dozen slack rope-ends
in each dream hand, tugging uselessly on memory
or hope. Frayed. She told stories. *I lived*
in Moscow once . . . *I nearly drowned* . . . Rotten.

Lightning struck me and I'm here to tell . . . Liar.
Hyperbole, falsehood, fiction, fib were pebbles
    tossed
at the evening's flat pool; her bright eyes
fixed on the ripples. No one believed her.
Our secret films are private affairs, watched
behind the eyes. She spoke in subtitles. Not on.

From bad to worse. The ambulance whinged all the
    way
to the park where she played with the stolen child.

You know the rest. The man in the long white wig who found her sadly confused. The top psychiatrist who studied her in gaol, then went back home and did what he does every night to the Princess of Wales.

Boy

I liked being small. When I'm on my own
I'm small. I put my pyjamas on
and hum to myself. I like doing that.

What I don't like is being large, you know,
grown-up. Just like that. Whoosh. Hairy.
I think of myself as a boy. Safe slippers.

The world is terror. Small you can go *As I
lay down my head to my sleep, I pray* . . . I remember
my three wishes sucked up a chimney of flame.

I can do it though. There was an older woman
who gave me a bath. She was joking, of course,
but I wasn't. I said *Mummy* to her. Off-guard.

Now it's a question of getting the wording right
for the Lonely Hearts verse. There must be someone
out there who's kind to boys. Even if they grew.

Eley's Bullet

Out walking in the fields, Eley found a bullet
with his name on it. Pheasants *korred*
and whirred at the sound of gunfire.
Eley's dog began to whine. England
was turning brown at the edges. Autumn. Rime
in the air. A cool bullet in his palm.

Eley went home. He put the tiny missile
in a matchbox and put that next to a pistol
in the drawer of his old desk. His dog
sat at his feet by the coal fire as he drank
a large whisky, then another one, but this
was usual. Eley went up the stairs to his bath.

He was in love with a woman in the town. The water
was just right, slid over his skin as he gave out
a long low satisfied moan into the steam.
His telephone began to ring and Eley cursed,
then dripped along the hall. She was in a call-box.
She'd lied all afternoon and tonight she was free.

The woman was married. Eley laughed aloud
with apprehension and delight, the world
expanded as he thought of her, his dog
trembled under his hand. Eley knelt,

he hugged the dog till it barked. Outside, the wind
knew something was on and nudged at the clouds.

They lay in each other's arms, as if what they had done
together had broken the pair of them. The woman
was half-asleep and Eley was telling himself
how he would spend a wish, if he could have only one
for the whole of his life. His fingers counted
the beads of her back as he talked in the dark.

At ten, Eley came into the bedroom with drinks.
She was combing her hair at the mirror. His eyes
seemed to hurt at the sight. She told him sorry,
but this was the last time. She tried to smile.
He stared, then said her words himself, the way
he'd spoken Latin as a boy. Dead language.

By midnight the moon was over the house, full
and lethal, and Eley alone. He went to his desk
with a bottle and started to write. Upstairs,
the dog sniffed at the tepid bed. Eley held
his head in his hands and wanted to cry,
but *Beloved* he wrote and *forever* and *why*.

Some men have no luck. Eley knew he'd as well
send her his ear as mail these stale words,
although he could taste her still. Nearby, a bullet
was there for the right moment and the right man.
He got out his gun, slowly, not even thinking,
and loaded it. Now he would choose. He paused.

He could finish the booze, sleep without dreams
with the morning to face, the loss of her
sore as the sunlight; or open his mouth
for a gun with his name on its bullet to roar
in his brains. Thunder or silence. Eley wished to God
he'd never loved. And then the frightened whimper of a dog.

Dream of a Lost Friend

You were dead, but we met, dreaming,
before you had died. Your name, twice,
then you turned, pale, unwell. *My dear,
my dear, must this be?* A public building
where I've never been, and, on the wall,
an AIDS poster. Your white lips. *Help me.*

We embraced, standing in a long corridor
which harboured a fierce pain neither of us felt yet.
The words you spoke were frenzied prayers
to Chemistry: or you laughed, a child-man's laugh,
innocent, hysterical, out of your skull. *It's only
a dream*, I heard myself saying, *only a bad dream.*

Some of our best friends nurture a virus, an idle,
charmed, purposeful enemy, and it dreams
they are dead already. In fashionable restaurants,
over the crudités, the healthy imagine a time
when all these careful moments will be dreamed
and dreamed again. *You look well. How do you feel?*

Then, as I slept, you backed away from me, crying
and offering a series of dates for lunch, waving.
I missed your funeral, I said, knowing you couldn't
     hear

at the end of the corridor, thumbs up, acting.
Where there's life . . . Awake, alive, for months I think of
  you
almost hopeful in a bad dream where you were long
  dead.

Who Loves You

I worry about you travelling in those mystical
    machines.
Every day people fall from the clouds, dead.
Breathe in and out and in and out easy.
Safety, safely, safe home.

Your photograph is in the fridge, smiles when the light
    comes on.
All the time people are burnt in the public places.
Rest where the cool trees drop to a gentle shade.
Safety, safely, safe home.

Don't lie down on the sands where the hole in the sky
    is.
Too many people being gnawed to shreds.
Send me your voice however it comes across oceans.
Safety, safely, safe home.

The loveless men and homeless boys are out there and
    angry.
Nightly people end their lives in the shortcut.
Walk in the light, steadily hurry towards me.
Safety, safely, safe home. (Who loves you?)
Safety, safely, safe home.

Girlfriends

derived from Verlaine
for John Griffith

That hot September night, we slept in a single bed,
naked, and on our frail bodies the sweat
cooled and renewed itself. I reached out my arms
and you, hands on my breasts, kissed me. Evening of
     amber.

Our nightgowns lay on the floor where you fell to your
     knees
and became ferocious, pressed your head to my
     stomach,
your mouth to the red gold, the pink shadows; except
I did not see it like this at the time, but arched

my back and squeezed water from the sultry air
with my fists. Also I remembered hearing, clearly
but distantly, a siren some streets away – *de*

da de da de da – which mingled with my own
absurd cries, so that I looked up, even then,
to see my fingers counting themselves, dancing.

Words, Wide Night

Somewhere on the other side of this wide night
and the distance between us, I am thinking of you.
The room is turning slowly away from the moon.

This is pleasurable. Or shall I cross that out and say
it is sad? In one of the tenses I singing
an impossible song of desire that you cannot hear.

La lala la. See? I close my eyes and imagine
the dark hills I would have to cross
to reach you. For I am in love with you and this

is what it is like or what it is like in words.

River

At the turn of the river the language changes,
a different babble, even a different name
for the same river. Water crosses the border,
translates itself, but words stumble, fall back,
and there, nailed to a tree, is proof. A sign

in new language brash on a tree. A bird,
not seen before, singing on a branch. A woman
on the path by the river, repeating a strange sound
to clue the bird's song and ask for its name, after.
She kneels for a red flower, picks it, later
will press it carefully between the pages of a book.

What would it mean to you if you could be
with her there, dangling your own hands in the water
where blue and silver fish dart away over stone,
stoon, stein, like the meanings of things, vanish?
She feels she is somewhere else, intensely, simply
    because
of words; sings loudly in nonsense, smiling, smiling.

If you were really there what would you write on a
    postcard,
or on the sand, near where the river runs into the sea?

The Way My Mother Speaks

I say her phrases to myself
in my head
or under the shallows of my breath,
restful shapes moving.
The day and ever. The day and ever.

The train this slow evening
goes down England
browsing for the right sky,
too blue swapped for a cool grey.
For miles I have been saying
What like is it
the way I say things when I think.
Nothing is silent. Nothing is not silent.
What like is it.

Only tonight
I am happy and sad
like a child
who stood at the end of summer
and dipped a net
in a green, erotic pond. *The day
and ever. The day and ever.*
I am homesick, free, in love
with the way my mother speaks.

In Your Mind

The other country, is it anticipated or half-remembered?
Its language is muffled by the rain which falls all
    afternoon
one autumn in England, and in your mind
you put aside your work and head for the airport
with a credit card and a warm coat you will leave
on the plane. The past fades like newsprint in the sun.

You know people there. Their faces are photographs
on the wrong side of your eyes. A beautiful boy
in the bar on the harbour serves you a drink – what? –
asks you if men could possibly land on the moon.
A moon like an orange drawn by a child. No.
Never. You watch it peel itself into the sea.

Sleep. The rasp of carpentry wakes you. On the wall,
a painting lost for thirty years renders the room yours.
Of course. You go to your job, right at the old hotel,
    left,
then left again. You love this job. Apt sounds
mark the passing of the hours. Seagulls. Bells. A flute
practising scales. You swap a coin for a fish on the way
    home.

Then suddenly you are lost but not lost, dawdling
on the blue bridge, watching six swans vanish
under your feet. The certainty of place turns on the
    lights
all over town, turns up the scent on the air. For a
    moment
you are there, in the other country, knowing its name.
And then a desk. A newspaper. A window. English
    rain.

From **Mean Time** (*1993*)

The Captain of the 1964 *Top of the Form* Team

Do Wah Diddy Diddy, Baby Love, Oh Pretty Woman
were in the Top Ten that month, October, and the Beatles
were everywhere else. I can give you the B-side
of the Supremes one. Hang on. *Come See About Me?*
I lived in a kind of fizzing hope. Gargling
with Vimto. The clever smell of my satchel. Convent
girls.
I pulled my hair forward with a steel comb that I blew
like Mick, my lips numb as a two-hour snog.

No snags. The Nile rises in April. Blue and White.
The humming-bird's song is made by its wings, which
beat
so fast that they blur in flight. I knew the capitals,
the Kings and Queens, the dates. In class, the white
sleeve
of my shirt saluted again and again. *Sir!* ... *Correct.*
Later, I whooped at the side of my bike, a cowboy,
mounted it running in one jump. I sped down Dyke
Hill,
no hands, famous, learning, *dominus domine dominum.*

Dave Dee Dozy ... Try me. Come on. My mother kept
my mascot Gonk
on the TV set for a year. And the photograph. I look

so brainy you'd think I'd just had a bath. The blazer.
The badge. The tie. The first chord of *A Hard Day's
    Night*
loud in my head. I ran to the Spinney in my prize shoes,
up Churchill Way, up Nelson Drive, over pink pavements
that girls chalked on, in a blue evening; and I stamped
the paw prints of badgers and skunks in the mud. My
    country.

I want it back. The Captain. The one with all the
    answers. *Bzz.*
My name was in red on Lucille Green's jotter. I smiled
as wide as a child who went missing on the way home
from school. The keeny. I say to my stale wife
Six hits by Dusty Springfield. I say to my boss *A pint!
How can we know the dancer from the dance?* Nobody.
My thick kids wince. *Name the Prime Minister of Rhodesia.*
My country. *How many florins in a pound?*

Litany

The soundtrack then was a litany – *candlewick*
bedspread three piece suite display cabinet –
and stiff-haired wives balanced their red smiles,
passing the catalogue. *Pyrex*. A tiny ladder
ran up Mrs Barr's American Tan leg, sly
like a rumour. Language embarrassed them.

The terrible marriages crackled, cellophane
round polyester shirts, and then The Lounge
would seem to bristle with eyes, hard
as the bright stones in engagement rings,
and sharp hands poised over biscuits as a word
was spelled out. An embarrassing word, broken

to bits, which tensed the air like an accident.
This was the code I learnt at my mother's knee,
    pretending
to read, where no one had cancer, or sex, or debts,
and certainly not leukaemia, which no one could
    spell.
The year a mass grave of wasps bobbed in a jam-jar;
a butterfly stammered itself in my curious hands.

A boy in the playground, I said, *told me*
to fuck off; and a thrilled, malicious pause

salted my tongue like an imminent storm. Then
uproar. *I'm sorry, Mrs Barr, Mrs Hunt, Mrs Emery,
sorry, Mrs Raine*. Yes, I can summon their names.
My mother's mute shame. The taste of soap.

Nostalgia

Those early mercenaries, it made them ill –
leaving the mountains, leaving the high, fine air
to go down, down. What they got
was money, dull crude coins clenched
in the teeth; strange food, the wrong taste,
stones in the belly; and the wrong sounds,
the wrong smells, the wrong light, every breath –
wrong. They had an ache *here*, Doctor,
they pined, wept, grown men. It was killing them.

It was given a name. Hearing tell of it,
there were those who stayed put, fearful
of a sweet pain in the heart; of how it hurt,
in that heavier air, to hear
the music of home – the sad pipes – summoning,
in the dwindling light of the plains,
a particular place – where maybe you met a girl,
or searched for a yellow ball in long grass,
found it just as your mother called you in.

But the word was out. Some would never
fall in love had they not heard of love.
So the priest stood at the stile with his head
in his hands, crying at the workings of memory
through the colour of leaves, and the schoolteacher

opened a book to the scent of her youth, too late.
It was spring when one returned, with his life
in a sack on his back, to find the same street
with the same sign on the inn, the same bell
chiming the hour on the clock, and everything changed.

Stafford Afternoons

Only there, the afternoons could suddenly pause
and when I looked up from lacing my shoe
a long road held no one, the gardens were empty,
an ice-cream van chimed and dwindled away.

On the motorway bridge, I waved at windscreens,
oddly hurt by the blurred waves back, the speed.
So I let a horse in the noisy field sponge at my palm
and invented, in colour, a vivid lie for us both.

In a cul-de-sac, a strange boy threw a stone.
I crawled through a hedge into long grass
at the edge of a small wood, lonely and thrilled.
The green silence gulped once and swallowed me
    whole.

I knew it was dangerous. The way the trees
drew sly faces from light and shade, the wood
let out its sticky breath on the back of my neck,
and flowering nettles gathered spit in their throats.

Too late. *Touch*, said the long-haired man
who stood, legs apart, by a silver birch
with a living, purple root in his hand. The sight
made sound rush back; birds, a distant lawnmower,

his hoarse, frightful endearments as I backed away
then ran all the way home; into a game
where children scattered and shrieked
and time fell from the sky like a red ball.

Brothers

Once, I slept in a bed with these four men who share
an older face and can be made to laugh, even now,
at random quotes from the play we were in. *There's no
      way
in the creation of God's earth*, I say. They grin and nod.

What was possible retreats and shrinks, and in my other
      eyes
they shrink to an altar boy, a boy practising scales,
a boy playing tennis with a wall, a baby
crying in the night like a new sound flailing for a shape.

Occasionally, when people ask, I enjoy reciting their
      names.
I don't have photographs, but I like to repeat the
      names.
My mother chose them. I hear her life in the words,
the breeding words, the word that broke her heart.

Much in common, me, with thieves and businessmen,
fathers and UB40s. We have nothing to say of now,
but time owns us. How tall they have grown. One day
I shall pay for a box and watch them shoulder it.

The Good Teachers

You run round the back to be in it again.
No bigger than your thumbs, those virtuous women
size you up from the front row. Soon now,
Miss Ross will take you for double History.
You breathe on the glass, making a ghost of her, say
South Sea Bubble Defenestration of Prague.

You love Miss Pirie. So much, you are top
of her class. So much, you need two of you
to stare out from the year, serious, passionate.
The River's Tale by Rudyard Kipling by heart.
Her kind intelligent green eye. Her cruel blue one.
You are making a poem up for her in your head.

But not Miss Sheridan. Comment vous appelez.
But not Miss Appleby. Equal to the square
of the other two sides. Never Miss Webb.
Dar es Salaam. Kilimanjaro. Look. The good teachers
swish down the corridor in long, brown skirts,
snobbish and proud and clean and qualified.

And they've got your number. You roll the waistband
of your skirt over and over, all leg, all
dumb insolence, smoke-rings. You won't pass.

You could do better. But there's the wall you climb
into dancing, lovebites, marriage, the Cheltenham
and Gloucester, today. The day you'll be sorry one day.

Like Earning a Living

What's an elephant like? I say
to the slack-mouthed girl
who answers back, a trainee ventriloquist,
then smirks at Donna. She dunno.
Nor does the youth with the face.
And what would that say, fingered?
I know. Video. Big Mac. Lager. Lager.
What like's a wart-hog? Come on.

Ambition. Rage. Boredom. Spite. How
do they taste, smell, sound?
Nobody cares. Jason doesn't. Nor does his dad.
He met a poet. Didn't know it. Uungh.
What would that aftershave say
if it could think? What colour's the future?

Somewhere in England, Major-Balls,
the long afternoon empties of air, meaning, energy,
    point.
Kin-L. There just aren't the words for it.
Darren. Paul. Kelly. Marie. What's it like? Mike?

Like earning a living.
Earning a living like.

Caul

No, I don't remember the thing itself.
I remember the word.
Amnion, inner membrane, *caul*.
I'll never be drowned.

The past is the future waiting for dreams
and will find itself there.
I came in a cloak of cool luck
and smiled at the world.

Where the man asked the woman to tell
how it felt, how it looked,
and a sailor purchased my charm
to bear to the sea.

I imagine it now, a leathery sheath
the length of a palm
empty as mine, under the waves
or spoil on a beach.

I'm all that is left of then. It spools
itself out like a film
a talented friend can recall
using speech alone.

The light of a candle seen in a caul
eased from my crown that day,
when all but this living noun
was taken away.

Away and See

Away and see an ocean suck at a boiled sun
and say to someone things I'd blush even to dream.
Slip off your dress in a high room over the harbour.
Write to me soon.

New fruits sing on the flipside of night in a market
of language, light, a tune from the chapel nearby
stopping you dead, the peach in your palm respiring.
Taste it for me.

Away and see the things that words give a name to, the
    flight
of syllables, wingspan stretching a noun. Test words
wherever they live; listen and touch, smell, believe.
Spell them with love.

Skedaddle. Somebody chaps at the door at a year's end,
    hopeful.
Away and see who it is. Let in the new, the vivid,
horror and pity, passion, the stranger holding the
    future.
Ask him his name.

Nothing's the same as anything else. Away and see
for yourself. Walk. Fly. Take a boat till land reappears,
altered for ever, ringing its bells, alive. Go on. G'on.
   Gon.
Away and see.

Small Female Skull

With some surprise, I balance my small female skull in
    my hands.
What is it like? An ocarina? Blow in its eye.
It cannot cry, holds my breath only as long as I exhale,
mildly alarmed now, into the hole where the nose was,
press my ear to its grin. A vanishing sigh.

For some time, I sit on the lavatory seat with my head
in my hands, appalled. It feels much lighter than I'd
    thought;
the weight of a deck of cards, a slim volume of verse,
but with something else, as though it could levitate.
    Disturbing.
So why do I kiss it on the brow, my warm lips to its
    papery bone,

and take it to the mirror to ask for a gottle of geer?
I rinse it under the tap, watch dust run away, like sand
from a swimming-cap, then dry it – firstborn – gently
with a towel. I see the scar where I fell for sheer love
down treacherous stairs, and read that shattering day
    like braille.

Love, I murmur to my skull, then, louder, other
    grand words,
shouting the hollow nouns in a white-tiled room.
Downstairs they will think I have lost my mind. No. I
    only weep
into these two holes here, or I'm grinning back at the
    joke, this is
a friend of mine. See, I hold her face in trembling,
    passionate hands.

Moments of Grace

I dream through a wordless, familiar place.
The small boat of the day sails into morning,
past the postman with his modest haul, the full trees
which sound like the sea, leaving my hands free
to remember. Moments of grace. *Like this*.

Shaken by first love and kissing a wall. *Of course*.
The dried ink on the palms then ran suddenly wet,
a glistening blue name in each fist. I sit now
in a kind of sly trance, hoping I will not feel me
breathing too close across time. A face to the name.
　Gone.

The chimes of mothers calling in children
at dusk. *Yes*. It seems we live in those staggering years
only to haunt them; the vanishing scents
and colours of infinite hours like a melting balloon
in earlier hands. The boredom since.

Memory's caged bird won't fly. These days
we are adjectives, nouns. In moments of grace
we were verbs, the secret of poems, talented.
A thin skin lies on the language. We stare
deep in the eyes of strangers, look for the doing words.

Now I smell you peeling an orange in the other room.
Now I take off my watch, let a minute unravel
in my hands, listen and look as I do so,
and mild loss opens my lips like *No*.
Passing, you kiss the back of my neck. A blessing.

The Grammar of Light

Even barely enough light to find a mouth,
and bless both with a meaningless O, teaches,
spells out. The way a curtain opened at night
lets in neon, or moon, or a car's hasty glance,
and paints for a moment someone you love, pierces.

And so many mornings to learn; some
when the day is wrung from damp, grey skies
and rooms come on for breakfast
in the town you are leaving early. The way
a wasteground weeps glass tears at the end of a
    street.

Some fluent, showing you how the trees
in the square think in birds, telepathise. The way
the waiter balances light in his hands, the coins
in his pocket silver, and a young bell shines
in its white tower ready to tell.

Even a saucer of rain in a garden at evening
speaks to the eye. Like the little fires
from allotments, undressing in veils of mauve smoke
as you walk home under the muted lamps,
perplexed. The way the shy stars go stuttering on.

And at midnight, a candle next to the wine
slurs its soft wax, flatters. Shadows
circle the table. The way all faces blur
to dreams of themselves held in the eyes.
The flare of another match. The way everything dies.

Valentine

Not a red rose or a satin heart.

I give you an onion.
It is a moon wrapped in brown paper.
It promises light
like the careful undressing of love.

Here.
It will blind you with tears
like a lover.
It will make your reflection
a wobbling photo of grief.

I am trying to be truthful.

Not a cute card or a kissogram.

I give you an onion.
Its fierce kiss will stay on your lips,
possessive and faithful
as we are,
for as long as we are.

Take it.
Its platinum loops shrink to a wedding-ring,
if you like.

Lethal.
Its scent will cling to your fingers,
cling to your knife.

Close

Lock the door. In the dark journey of our night,
two childhoods stand in the corner of the bedroom
watching the way we take each other to bits
to stare at our heart. I hear a story
told in sleep in a lost accent. You know the words.

Undress. A suitcase crammed with secrets
bursts in the wardrobe at the foot of the bed.
Dress again. Undress. You have me like a drawing,
erased, coloured in, untitled, signed by your
   tongue.
The name of a country written in red on my palm,

unreadable. I tell myself where I live now,
but you move in close till I shake, homeless,
further than that. A coin falls from the bedside table,
spinning its heads and tails. How the hell
can I win. How can I lose. Tell me again.

Love won't give in. It makes a hired room tremble
with the pity of bells, a cigarette smoke itself
next to a full glass of wine, time ache
into space, space, wants no more talk. Now
it has me where I want me, now you, you do.

Put out the light. Years stand outside on the street
looking up to an open window, black as our mouth
which utters its tuneless song. The ghosts of ourselves,
behind and before us, throng in a mirror, blind,
laughing and weeping. They know who we are.

Adultery

Wear dark glasses in the rain.
Regard what was unhurt
as though through a bruise.
Guilt. A sick, green tint.

New gloves, money tucked in the palms,
the handshake crackles. Hands
can do many things. Phone.
Open the wine. Wash themselves. Now

you are naked under your clothes all day,
slim with deceit. Only the once
brings you alone to your knees,
miming, more, more, older and sadder,

creative. Suck a lie with a hole in it
on the way home from a lethal, thrilling night
up against a wall, faster. Language
unpeels to a lost cry. You're a bastard.

Do it do it do it. Sweet darkness
in the afternoon; a voice in your ear
telling you how you are wanted,
which way, now. A telltale clock

wiping the hours from its face, your face
on a white sheet, gasping, radiant, yes.
Pay for it in cash, fiction, cab-fares back
to the life which crumbles like a wedding-cake.

Paranoia for lunch; too much
to drink, as a hand on your thigh
tilts the restaurant. You know all about love,
don't you. Turn on your beautiful eyes

for a stranger who's dynamite in bed, again
and again; a slow replay in the kitchen
where the slicing of innocent onions
scalds you to tears. Then, selfish autobiographical sleep

in a marital bed, the tarnished spoon of your body
stirring betrayal, your heart overripe at the core.
You're an expert, darling; your flowers
dumb and explicit on nobody's birthday.

So write the script – illness and debt,
a ring thrown away in a garden
no moon can heal, your own words
commuting to bile in your mouth, terror –

and all for the same thing twice. And all
for the same thing twice. You did it.
What. Didn't you. Fuck. Fuck. No. That was
the wrong verb. This is only an abstract noun.

Fraud

Firstly, I changed my name
to that of a youth I knew for sure had bought it in
   1940, Rotterdam.
Private M.
I was my own poem,
pseudonym,
rule of thumb.
What was my aim?
To change from a bum
to a billionaire. I spoke the English. Mine was a scam
involving pensions, papers, politicians in-and-out of
   their pram.
And I was to blame.

For what? There's a gnome
in Zurich knows more than people assume.
There's a military man, Jerusalem
way, keeping schtum.
Then there's Him –
for whom
I paid for a butch and femme
to make him come.
And all of the crème
de la crème
considerd me scum.

Poverty's dumb.
Take it from me, Sonny Jim,
learn to lie in the mother-tongue of the motherfucker
    you want to charm.
They're all the same,
turning their wide blind eyes to crime.
And who gives a damn
when the keys to a second home
are pressed in his palm,
or Polaroids of a Night of Shame
with a Boy on the Game
are passed his way at the A.G.M.?

So read my lips. Mo-ney. Pow-er. Fame.
And had I been asked, in my time,
in my puce and prosperous prime,
if I recalled the crumbling slum
of my Daddy's home,
if I was a shit, a sham,
if I'd done immeasurable harm,
I could have replied with a dream:
the water that night was calm
and with my enormous mouth, in bubbles and blood
    and phlegm,
I gargled my name.

The Biographer

Because you are dead,
I stand at your desk,
my fingers caressing the grooves in the wood
your initials made;
and I manage a quote,
echo one of your lines in the small, blue room
where an early daguerreotype shows you
excitedly staring out
from behind your face,
the thing that made you yourself
still visibly there,
like a hood and a cloak of light.
The first four words that I write are your name.

I'm a passionate man
with a big advance
who's loved your work since he was a boy;
but the night
I slept alone in your bed,
the end of a fire going out in the grate,
I came awake –
certain, had we ever met,
you wouldn't have wanted me,
or needed me,

would barely have noticed me at all.
Guilt and rage
hardened me then,
and later I felt your dislike
chilling the air
as I drifted away.
Your wallpaper green and crimson and gold.

How close can I get
to the sound of your voice
which Emma Elizabeth Hibbert described –
lively, eager and lightly-pitched,
with none of the later, bitter edge.
Cockney, a little.
In London Town,
the faces you wrote
leer and gape and plead at my feet.
Once, high on Hungerford Bridge,
a stew and tangle of rags, sniffed by a dog, stood,
    spoke,
spat at the shadow I cast,
at the meagre shadow I cast in my time.
I heard the faraway bells of St Paul's as I ran.

Maestro. Monster. Mummy's Boy.
My Main Man.
I write you and write you for five hard years.
I have an affair with a thespian girl –
you would have approved –
then I snivel home to my wife.
Her poems and jam.

Her forgiveness.
Her violent love.
And this is a life.
I print it out.
I print it out.
In all of your mirrors, my face;
with its smallish, its quizzical eyes,
its cheekbones, its sexy jaw,
its talentless, dustjacket smile.

Mean Time

The clocks slid back an hour
and stole light from my life
as I walked through the wrong part of town,
mourning our love.

And, of course, unmendable rain
fell to the bleak streets
where I felt my heart gnaw
at all our mistakes.

If the darkening sky could lift
more than one hour from this day
there are words I would never have said
nor have heard you say.

But we will be dead, as we know,
beyond all light.
These are the shortened days
and the endless nights.

Prayer

Some days, although we cannot pray, a prayer
utters itself. So, a woman will lift
her head from the sieve of her hands and stare
at the minims sung by a tree, a sudden gift.

Some nights, although we are faithless, the truth
enters our hearts, that small familiar pain;
then a man will stand stock-still, hearing his youth
in the distant Latin chanting of a train.

Pray for us now. Grade I piano scales
console the lodger looking out across
a Midlands town. Then dusk, and someone calls
a child's name as though they named their loss.

Darkness outside. Inside, the radio's prayer –
Rockall. Malin. Dogger. Finisterre.

From **The World's Wife** (*1999*)

Mrs Midas

It was late September. I'd just poured a glass of wine, begun
to unwind, while the vegetables cooked. The kitchen
filled with the smell of itself, relaxed, its steamy breath
gently blanching the windows. So I opened one,
then with my fingers wiped the other's glass like a brow.
He was standing under the pear-tree snapping a twig.

Now the garden was long and the visibility poor, the way
the dark of the ground seems to drink the light of the sky,
but that twig in his hand was gold. And then he plucked
a pear from a branch, we grew Fondante d'Automne,
and it sat in his palm like a light-bulb. On.
I thought to myself, Is he putting fairy lights in the tree?

He came into the house. The doorknobs gleamed.
He drew the blinds. You know the mind; I thought of
the Field of the Cloth of Gold and of Miss Macready.
He sat in that chair like a king on a burnished throne.

The look on his face was strange, wild, vain; I said,
What in the name of God is going on? He started to
    laugh.

I served up the meal. For starters, corn on the cob.
Within seconds he was spitting out the teeth of the rich.
He toyed with his spoon, then mine, then with the
    knives, the forks.
He asked where was the wine. I poured with a shaking
    hand,
a fragrant, bone-dry white from Italy, then watched
as he picked up the glass, goblet, golden chalice, drank.

It was then that I started to scream. He sank to his
    knees.
After we'd both calmed down, I finished the wine
on my own, hearing him out. I made him sit
on the other side of the room and keep his hands to
    himself.
I locked the cat in the cellar. I moved the phone.
The toilet I didn't mind. I couldn't believe my ears:

how he'd had a wish. Look, we all have wishes;
    granted.
But who has wishes granted? Him. Do you know about
    gold?
It feeds no one; aurum, soft, untarnishable; slakes
no thirst. He tried to light a cigarette; I gazed, entranced,
as the blue flame played on its luteous stem. At least,
I said, you'll be able to give up smoking for good.

Separate beds. In fact, I put a chair against my door,
near petrified. He was below, turning the spare room
into the tomb of Tutankhamen. You see, we were
    passionate then,
in those halcyon days; unwrapping each other, rapidly,
like presents, fast food. But now I feared his honeyed
    embrace,
the kiss that would turn my lips to a work of art.

And who, when it comes to the crunch, can live
with a heart of gold? That night, I dreamt I bore
his child, its perfect ore limbs, its little tongue
like a precious latch, its amber eyes
holding their pupils like flies. My dream-milk
burned in my breasts. I woke to the streaming sun.

So he had to move out. We'd a caravan
in the wilds, in a glade of its own. I drove him up
under cover of dark. He sat in the back.
And then I came home, the woman who married the
    fool
who wished for gold. At first I visited, odd times,
parking the car a good way off, then walking.

You knew you were getting close. Golden trout
on the grass. One day, a hare hung from a larch,
a beautiful lemon mistake. And then his footprints,
glistening next to the river's path. He was thin,
delirious; hearing, he said, the music of Pan
from the woods. Listen. That was the last straw.

What gets me now is not the idiocy or greed
but lack of thought for me. Pure selfishness. I sold
the contents of the house and came down here.
I think of him in certain lights, dawn, late afternoon,
and once a bowl of apples stopped me dead. I miss
    most,
even now, his hands, his warm hands on my skin, his
    touch.

Mrs Lazarus

I had grieved. I had wept for a night and a day
over my loss, ripped the cloth I was married in
from my breasts, howled, shrieked, clawed
at the burial stones till my hands bled, retched
his name over and over again, dead, dead.

Gone home. Gutted the place. Slept in a single cot,
widow, one empty glove, white femur
in the dust, half. Stuffed dark suits
into black bags, shuffled in a dead man's shoes,
noosed the double knot of a tie round my bare neck,

gaunt nun in the mirror, touching herself. I learnt
the Stations of Bereavement, the icon of my face
in each bleak frame; but all those months
he was going away from me, dwindling
to the shrunk size of a snapshot, going,

going. Till his name was no longer a certain spell
for his face. The last hair on his head
floated out from a book. His scent went from the
    house.
The will was read. See, he was vanishing
to the small zero held by the gold of my ring.

Then he was gone. Then he was legend, language;
my arm on the arm of the schoolteacher – the shock
of a man's strength under the sleeve of his coat –
along the hedgerows. But I was faithful
for as long as it took. Until he was memory.

So I could stand that evening in the field
in a shawl of fine air, healed, able
to watch the edge of the moon occur to the sky
and a hare thump from a hedge; then notice
the village men running towards me, shouting,

behind them the women and children, barking dogs,
and I knew. I knew by the shrill light
on the blacksmith's face, the sly eyes
of the barmaid, the sudden hands bearing me
into the hot tang of the crowd parting before me.

He lived. I saw the horror on his face.
I heard his mother's crazy song. I breathed
his stench; my bridegroom in his rotting shroud,
moist and dishevelled from the grave's slack chew,
croaking his cuckold name, disinherited, out of his
     time.

From **Mrs Tiresias**

All I know is this:
he went out for his walk a man
and came home female.

Out the back gate with his stick,
the dog;
wearing his gardening kecks,
an open-necked shirt,
and a jacket in Harris tweed I'd patched at the elbows
    myself.

Whistling.

He liked to hear
the first cuckoo of Spring
then write to the *Times*.
I'd usually heard it
days before him
but I never let on.

I'd heard one that morning
while he was asleep;
just as I heard,
at about 6pm,
a faint sneer of thunder up in the woods
and felt

a sudden heat
at the back of my knees.

He was late getting back.

I was brushing my hair at the mirror
and running a bath
when a face
swam into view
next to my own.

The eyes were the same.
But in the shocking V of the shirt were breasts.
When he uttered my name in his woman's voice I passed
    out.

               *

Life has to go on.

I put it about that he was a twin
and this was his sister
come down to live
while he himself
was working abroad.

And at first I tried to be kind;
blow-drying his hair till he learnt to do it himself,
lending him clothes till he started to shop for his own,
sisterly, holding his soft new shape in my arms all
    night.

Then he started his period.

One week in bed.
Two doctors in.
Three painkillers four times a day.

And later
a letter
to the powers-that-be
demanding full-paid menstrual leave twelve weeks per
    year.
I see him now,
his selfish pale face peering at the moon
through the bathroom window.
The curse, he said, *the curse.*

Don't kiss me in public,
he snapped the next day,
I don't want people getting the wrong idea.

It got worse.

*

After he left, I would glimpse him
out and about,
entering glitzy restaurants
on the arms of powerful men –
though I knew for sure
there'd be nothing of *that*
going on
if he had his way –
or on TV
telling the women out there

how, as a woman himself,
he knew how we felt.

His flirt's smile.

The one thing he never got right
was the voice.
A cling-peach slithering out from its tin.

I gritted my teeth.

*

And this is my lover, I said,
the one time we met,
at a glittering ball,
under the lights,
among tinkling glass,
and watched the way he stared
at her violet eyes,
at the blaze of her skin,
at the slow caress of her hand on the back of my neck;
and saw him picture
her bite,
her bite at the fruit of my lips,
and hear
my red wet cry in the night
as she shook his hand
saying *How do you do*;
and I noticed then his hands, her hands,
the clash of their sparkling rings and their painted nails.

Mrs Aesop

By Christ, he could bore for Purgatory. He was small,
didn't prepossess. So he tried to impress. *Dead men,
Mrs Aesop*, he'd say, *tell no tales*. Well, let me tell you
    now
that the bird in his hand shat on his sleeve,
never mind the two worth less in the bush. Tedious.

Going out was worst. He'd stand at our gate, look,
    then leap;
scour the hedgerows for a shy mouse, the fields
for a sly fox, the sky for one particular swallow
    that couldn't make a summer. The jackdaw, according
    to him,
envied the eagle. Donkeys would, on the whole, prefer
    to be lions.

On one appalling evening stroll, we passed an old hare
snoozing in a ditch – he stopped and made a note –
and then, about a mile further on, a tortoise, somebody's
    pet,
creeping, slow as marriage, up the road. *Slow
but certain, Mrs Aesop, wins the race*. Asshole.

What race? What sour grapes? What silk purse,
sow's ear, dog in a manger, what big fish? Some days,
I could barely keep awake as the story droned on

towards the moral of itself. *Action, Mrs A., speaks louder than words*. And that's another thing, the sex

was diabolical. I gave him a fable one night
about a little cock that wouldn't crow, a razor-sharp axe
with a heart blacker than the pot that called the kettle.
I'll cut off your tail, all right, I said, *to save my face*.
That shut him up. I laughed last, longest.

Queen Kong

I remember peeping in at his skyscraper room
and seeing him fast asleep. My little man.
I'd been in Manhattan a week,
making my plans; staying at 2 quiet hotels
in the Village, where people were used to strangers
and more or less left you alone. To this day,
I'm especially fond of pastrami on rye.

I digress. As you see, this island's a paradise.
He'd arrived, my man, with a documentary team
to make a film. (There's a particular toad
that lays its eggs only here.) I found him alone
in a clearing, scooped him up in my palm,
and held his wriggling, shouting life till he calmed.
For me, it was absolutely love at first sight.

I'd been so *lonely*. Long nights in the heat
of my own pelt, rumbling an animal blues.
All right, he was small, but perfectly formed
and *gorgeous*. There were things he could do
for me with the sweet finesse of those hands
that no gorilla could. I swore in my huge heart
to follow him then to the ends of the earth.

For he wouldn't stay here. He was nervous.
I'd go to his camp each night at dusk,
crouch by the delicate tents, and wait. His colleagues
always sent him out pretty quick. He'd climb
into my open hand, sit down; and then I'd gently pick
at his shirt and his trews, peel him, put
the tip of my tongue to the grape of his flesh.

Bliss. But when he'd finished his prize-winning film,
he packed his case; hopped up and down
on my heartline, miming the flight back home
to New York. *Big metal bird.* Didn't he know
I could swat his plane from these skies like a gnat?
But I let him go, my man. I watched him fly
into the sun as I thumped at my breast, distraught.

I lasted a month. I slept for a week,
then woke to binge for a fortnight. I didn't wash.
The parrots clacked their migraine chant.
The swinging monkeys whinged. Fevered, I drank
handfuls of river right by the spot where he'd bathed.
I bled when a fat, red moon rolled on the jungle roof.
And after that, I decided to get him back.

So I came to sail up the Hudson one June night,
with the New York skyline a concrete rain-forest
of light; and felt, lovesick and vast, the first
glimmer of hope in weeks. I was discreet, prowled
those streets in darkness; pressing my passionate eye
to a thousand windows, each with its modest peep-show
of boredom or pain, of drama, consolation, remorse.

I found him, of course, At 3am on a Sunday,
dreaming alone in his single bed; over his lovely head,
a blown-up photograph of myself. I stared for a long
    time
till my big brown eyes grew moist, then I padded
    away
through Central Park, under the stars. He was mine.
Next day, I shopped. Clothes for my man, mainly,
but one or two treats for myself from Bloomingdale's.

I picked him, like a chocolate from the top layer
of a box, one Friday night, out of his room;
and let him dangle in the air between my finger
and my thumb in a teasing, lover's way. Then we sat
on the tip of the Empire State Building, saying farewell
to the Brooklyn Bridge, to the winking yellow cabs,
to the helicopters over the river, dragonflies.

Twelve happy years. He slept in my fur; woke
    early
to massage the heavy lids of my eyes. I liked that.
He liked me to gently blow on him; or scratch,
with care, the length of his back with my nail.
Then I'd ask him to play on the wooden pipes he
    made
in our first year. He'd sit, cross-legged, near my ear
for hours; his plaintive, lost tunes making me cry.

When he died, I held him all night, shaking him
like a doll, licking his face, breast, soles of his feet,
his little rod. But then, heartsore as I was, I set to
    work.

He would be pleased. I wear him now, about my neck,
perfect, preserved, with tiny emeralds for eyes. No man
has been loved more. I'm sure that, sometimes, in his
    silent death,
against my massive, breathing lungs, he hears me roar.

Mrs Darwin

7 April 1852.
Went to the Zoo.
I said to Him –
Something about that Chimpanzee over there reminds
   me of you.

SELECTED POEMS

JAMES FENTON

This is the first full selection of James Fenton's poems to be published, and represents the whole range of his work from light verse to political and love poems to opera libretti. It includes early work from *The Memory of War* and *Children in Exile* as well as later work from *Out of Danger,* which won the Whitbread Poetry Prize in 1994. Also represented are examples of his work in verse for the stage and recent unpublished poems.

'Passionate and personal; Fenton's poems can also be extremely funny and violent; they are always full of the pleasures of the language' Paul Theroux

'Fenton is very popular – it's the way he writes, with a mixture of poetic language and real directness' Peter Porter

'For my money, *Out of Danger* is one of the best collections of the past twenty years' Giles Foden, *Guardian*

'A brilliant poet of technical virtuosity' Stephen Spender

'The most talented poet of his generation' *Observer*

SELECTED POEMS

ROGER MCGOUGH

Selected Poems consists of work chosen by the poet himself from *Collected Poems*, published by Penguin in 2004, together with several new, previously unpublished poems. The complete span of McGough's writing, from the 1960s to the new millennium, is represented.

'McGough is a true original and more than one generation would be much the poorer without him' *The Times*

'Memorable and enduring and fresh. Age has not withered [his lines] nor diminished his potency. Of how much modern poetry can you say that?' *Sunday Herald*

'Over forty years ago, this shy Liverpudlian asked Poetry if it was dancing. Since then we have all, readers and poets alike, come out of the hushed libraries and the solemn universities to join in the party. We are lucky indeed to have him' Carol Ann Duffy

'McGough has done for British poetry what champagne does for weddings' *Time Out*

'No detail of daily life, trivial, ridiculous or touching, is unworthy of sympathetic attention … honest, enlivening' Alan Brownjohn, *Sunday Times*

SELECTED POEMS

TONY HARRISON

This generous selection of Tony Harrison's poems includes sixty-three poems from his famous sonnet sequence *The School of Eloquence* and the remarkable long poem 'v.', a meditation in a vandalized Leeds graveyard, written during the miners' strike, which created such a stir when it was broadcast on television in the late 1980s.

'A voracious appetite for language. Brilliant, passionate, outrageous, abrasive, but also, as in the family sonnets, immeasurably tender' Harold Pinter

'Reaffirms his place in the front rank of contemporary British poets … His range is exhilarating, his clarity and technical mastery a sharp pleasure' Melvyn Bragg

'The poem "v." is the most outstanding social poem of the last twenty-five years . . . Seldom has a British poem of such personal intensity had such a universal range' Martin Booth

'More than any other English poet I have read in recent years, Harrison makes good Camus's claim that the function of art is "to open the prisons and give a voice to the sorrows and joys of all" ' John Lucas, *New Statesman*

'Poems written in a style which I fell I have all my life been waiting for' Stephen Spender

SELECTED POEMS

If you enjoyed this book, there are several ways you can read more by the same author and make sure you get the inside track on all Penguin books.

Order any of the following titles direct:

0141025123	CAROL ANN DUFFY	£8.99

'In the world of British poetry, Carol Ann Duffy is a superstar. Highbrow and lowbrow, readers love her' *Guardian*

0141023228	ROGER MCGOUGH	£8.99

'McGough has done for British poetry what champagne does for weddings' *Time Out*

0141024410	JAMES FENTON	£8.99

'The most talented poet of his generation' *Observer*

From 1st June 2006:

0141025018	LINTON KWESI JOHNSON	£8.99

'Linton's rhymes speak for our times' *The Voice*

014102609X	DEREK MAHON	£8.99

'Required reading for anyone interested in contemporary poetry' Grey Gowrie

0141026073	SOPHIE HANNAH	£8.99

'The brightest young star in British poetry' *Independent*

014102500X	GEOFFREY HILL	£8.99

'England's most important living poet' *The Times*

Simply call Penguin c/o Bookpost on **01624 677237** and have your credit/debit card ready. Alternatively e-mail your order to **bookshop@enterprise.net**. Postage and package is free in mainland UK. Overseas customers must add £2 per book. Prices and availability subject to change without notice.

Visit www.penguin.com and find out first about forthcoming titles, read exclusive material and author interviews, and enter exciting competitions. You can also browse through thousands of Penguin books and buy online.

IT'S NEVER BEEN EASIER TO READ MORE WITH PENGUIN

Frustrated by the quality of books available at Exeter station for his journey back to London one day in 1935, Allen Lane decided to do something about it. The Penguin paperback was born that day, and with it first-class writing became available to a mass audience for the very first time. This book is a direct descendant of those original Penguins and Lane's momentous vision. What will you read next?